made in
france

Agnès Delage-Calvet - Anne Sohier-Fournel

Muriel Brunet - Françoise Ritz

made in france

Cross stitch and embroidery in red, white and blue

Photography by Frédéric Lucano

Styling by Sonia Lucano

MURDOCH BOOKS

Contents

Introduction

Turn out your cupboards, sort through your drawers, check out your nearest embroidery shop and have a go!
Everything can be embroidered — from little canvas shoes to bed linen and handkerchiefs, from linen bags to bath towels and cotton tea towels.
Some simple and charming motifs, a skein or two of embroidery thread, a needle and a few basic stitches — nothing could be simpler.
Follow the advice and tips on pages 9 to 13 and let yourself be seduced by the simple art of embroidery.

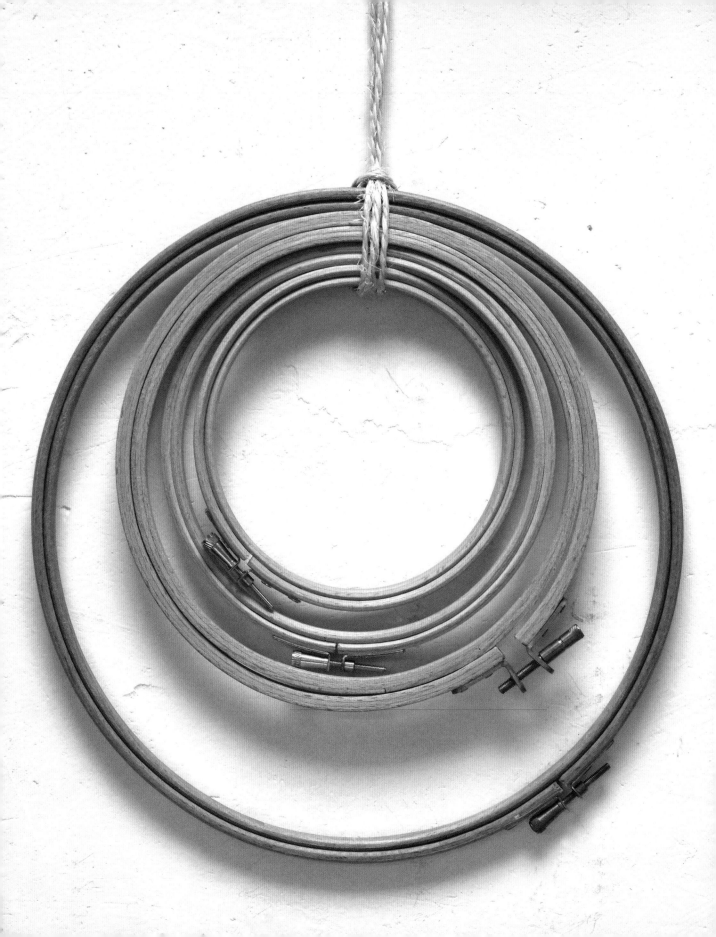

Getting started

Before starting to embroider,

make sure that your fabric is prepared, so that it doesn't fray during the course of your work. You can either oversew the edges with large basting stitches or, more simply, bind the edges with low-tack masking tape. Your fabric should always be somewhat larger than the motif that you're going to embroider.

Fold the fabric in quarters to find the centre point. Use large basting stitches to mark the horizontal and vertical fold lines, which will serve as a guide to positioning your motif. On the cross stitch charts, find the centre stitch of the design you have chosen and begin your embroidery at this point, working the centre stitch at the centre point of the fabric. When the embroidery is complete, remove the basting threads.

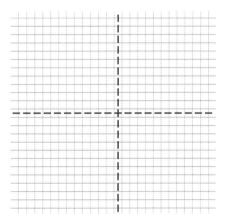

To maintain an even tension in your stitches, use an embroidery hoop. Stretch your fabric in the hoop, but take care to remove it frequently, to avoid permanently damaging the weave of the fabric.

Make a small sample piece of several stitches to determine the number of embroidery threads that will suit the weight of the fabric you are using. This sample piece is a good idea for all types of embroidery. Stranded embroidery cotton is composed of six threads or strands. Cut your thread lengths to about 40cm. As a general rule, on 14-count Aida cloth, you would use 2 or 3 strands of thread; on 28- or 32-count linen, you would use 2 strands of thread over 2 threads of fabric. However, if you want to work over a single thread of linen, you should use one strand of thread.

When you begin, insert your needle into the fabric from the back and pull the thread through, leaving 2cm of thread at the back. When you work the first few stitches, catch the tail of thread under the stitches to secure it.

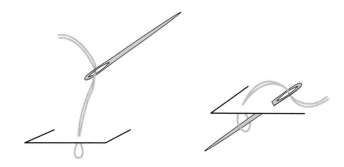

To finish a thread, take the needle to the back and slip it under the last 3 or 4 stitches. This method avoids making bulky knots on the back of your work.

To transfer the motif to your project,

use special embroiderer's carbon paper, which is available in several colours. Choose one that is appropriate for the fabric you are going to embroider. As a general rule, you should use white for dark fabric and blue or red for lighter coloured fabrics.

Photocopy your motif, enlarging it the desired size. Trace it onto tracing paper, following all the lines accurately and including all the details. Iron your fabric carefully and lay it on a smooth flat surface. Position the tracing paper on top.

Slip the carbon paper between the tracing paper and the fabric, carbon-side down, and secure the layers together with a couple of pins. With a pencil or biro, carefully trace over the outline and details of your motif, making sure that the whole design is transferred.

When you have finished transferring the motif, separate the layers carefully, taking care not to put any extra carbon marks on your fabric.

Before starting to embroider,

read all the stitching instructions - you'll find several tips to make your work easier.

Stitch library

To embroider the motifs and charts in this book,

you only need seven basic stitches, all very simple and easy to work.
The traditional embroidery designs are all worked mainly in stem stitch. Where
a different stitch is used for a detail, it is indicated on the individual design.

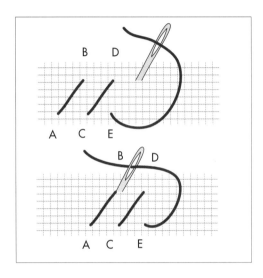

Cross stitch

1/ Bring the needle out at A, back in at B
and out again at C. Take it in again at D,
then out again at E.

2/ Work in reverse to complete the row
of crosses. From E back to B forms one cross.

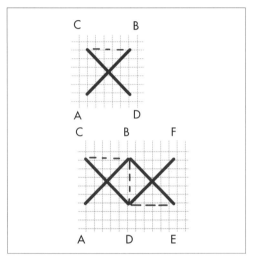

Cross stitch (alternate method)

1/ Bring the needle out at A, back in at B,
out again at C, then in at D.

2/ Bring it out again at B, back in at E,
out again at D, then in at F,
to form complete crosses, one at a time.

The thread at the back of the work forms
a squared-off zigzag.

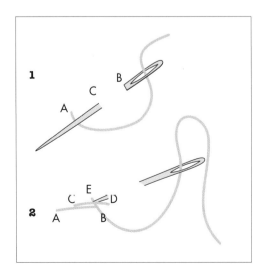

Stem stitch

1/ Bring the needle out at A and reinsert it at B.
Bring it out again at C, halfway between A and B.
Keep the thread below the needle.

2/ Insert the needle at D and bring it out again
at B, keeping the thread above the needle.
Insert the needle at E and bring it out again at D,
with the thread below the needle.

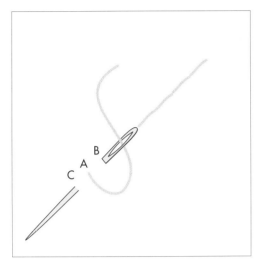

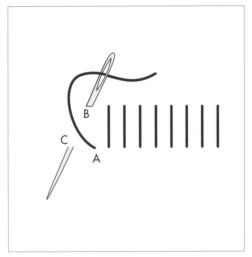

Back stitch

Bring the needle out at A and reinsert it at B.
Bring it out again at C. The stitch AB should be
the same length as the stitch AC.

Straight stitch

Bring the needle out at A, reinsert it at B
and bring it out again at C. Do not make
the stitch too long – rather, make two stitches,
one after the other.

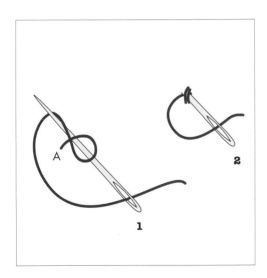

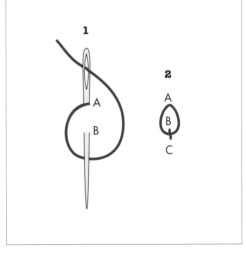

French knot

1/ Bring the needle out at A. Pull the thread taut
and wrap it twice around the needle.

2/ Without releasing the thread, reinsert the
needle at A, pulling the thread through
and holding the loops with your finger until
a knot is formed.

Detached chain stitch

1/ Bring the needle out at A. Make a loop and
reinsert the needle again at A.

2/ Bring the needle out at B, through the loop,
and reinsert it at C, just below B, to make a tiny
holding stitch for the loop.

red

1. Embroidered sampler
/ motifs page 37

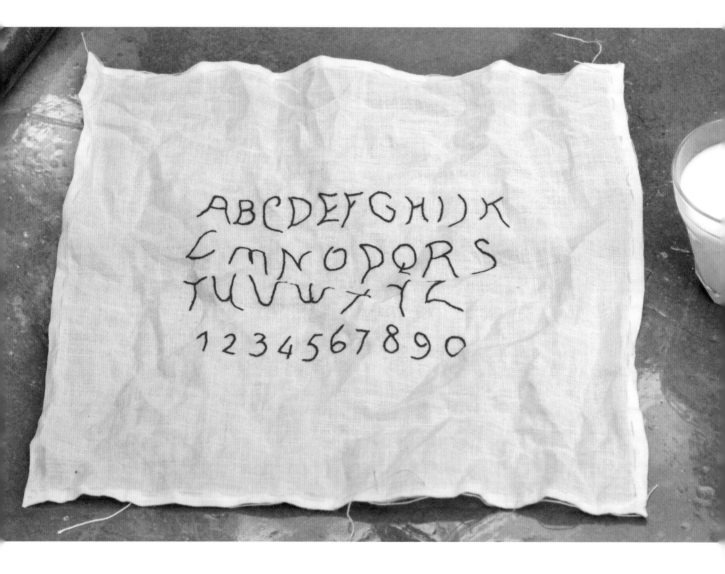

2. Child's pillowcase
/ motifs pages 38-39

THE NEW
REAL BOOK

Jazz Classics
Choice Standards
Pop-Fusion Classics

3. Shopping bag
/ motifs pages 40-41

4. Picnic cloth
/ motifs pages 42-43

5. Garden apron
/ motifs page 44

6. Tea cloth

/ motifs page 45

7. Tank top / motifs pages 46-47

8. Holiday napkins
/ motifs pages 48-49

9. Runner
/ motifs page 50

10. Satchel
/ motifs page 51

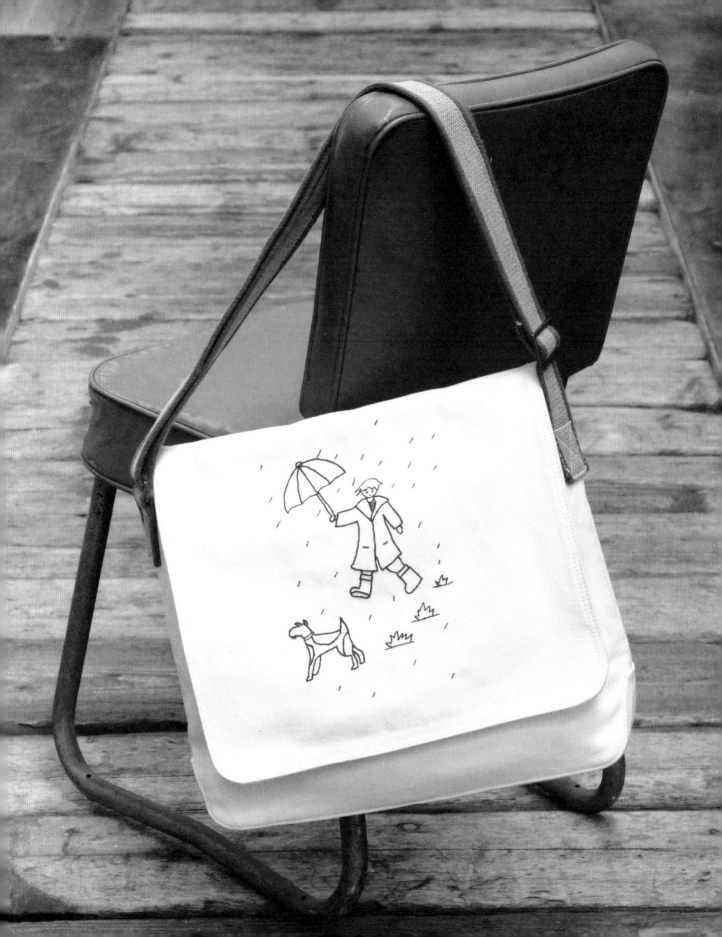

11. Recipe book
/ motifs page 52

12. Cross stitch tea towel
/ motifs pages 53

13. Child's dress
/ motifs page 54

14. Romantic sheet
/ motifs page 55

15. Cross stitch bath towels
/ motifs pages 56-57

16. Throw
/ motifs pages 58-59

33

17. European cushion cover
/ motifs pages 60-61

18. Christmas decoration
/ motifs pages 62-63

ABCDEFGHIJK
LMNOPQRS
TUVWXYZ
1234567890

ABCDEFGHIJ
KLMNOPQRS
TUVWXYZ
1234567890

2. Child's pillowcase
/ photo page 17

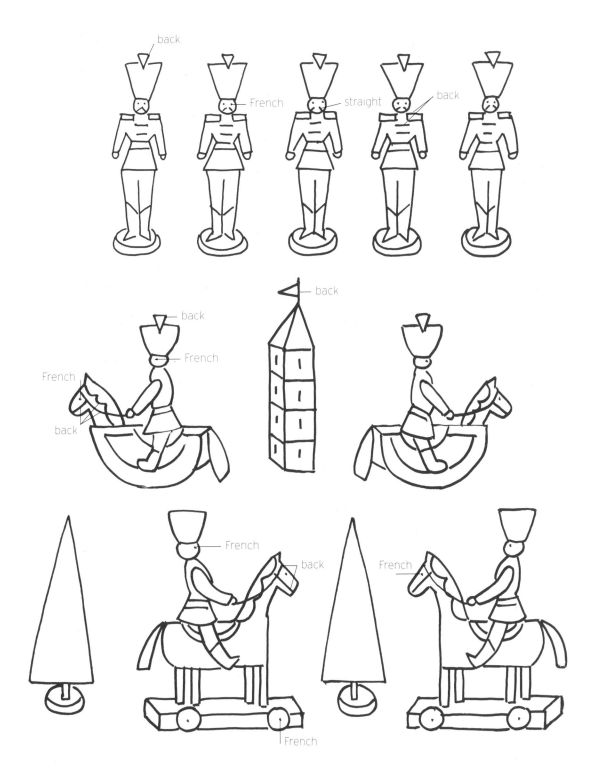

3. Shopping bag / photo page 18

4. Picnic cloth

/ photo page 19

5. Garden Apron

/ photo page 20

6. Tea cloth

/ photo page 21

detached

straight

back

7. Tank top

/ photo pages 22-23

9. Runner
/ photo page 26

French

back

detached

back

French

back

back

back

15. Cross stitch bath towels

/ photo page 32

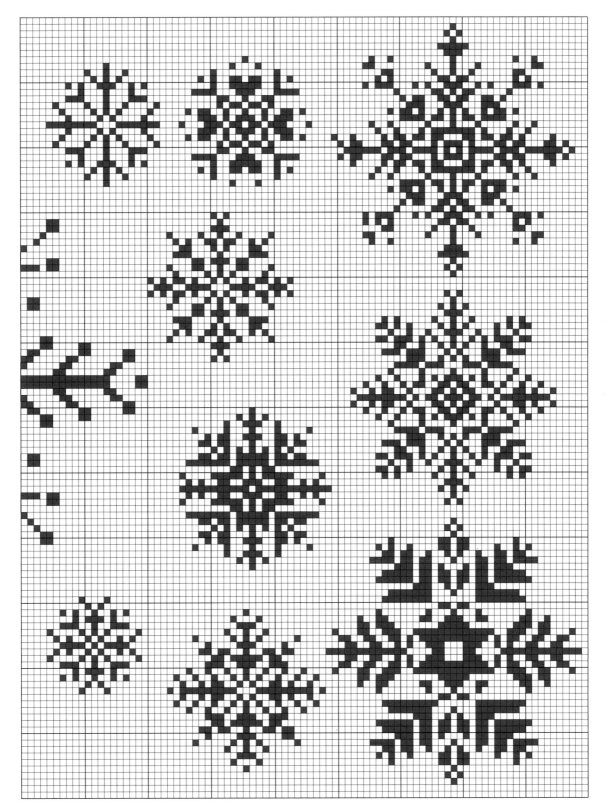

16. Throw
/ photo page 33

/ photo page 34

18. Christmas decoration

/ photo page 35

white

19. Marriage sampler
/ motifs pages 88-91

20. Pot cover
/ motifs pages 90-91

21. Good luck cushions / motifs pages 92-93

22. Secret notebook / motifs pages 94-95

24. Jacket
/ motifs page 97

25. Stole
/ motifs page 98

Atelier

26. Lampshade
/ motifs page 99

27. Lingerie bag
/ motifs pages 100-101

28. Plant markers
/ motifs pages 102-103

29. Embroiderer's keepsakes

/ motifs pages 104-105

30. Monogrammed tea towels
/ motifs pages 106-107

31. Kitchen apron
/ motifs pages 108-109

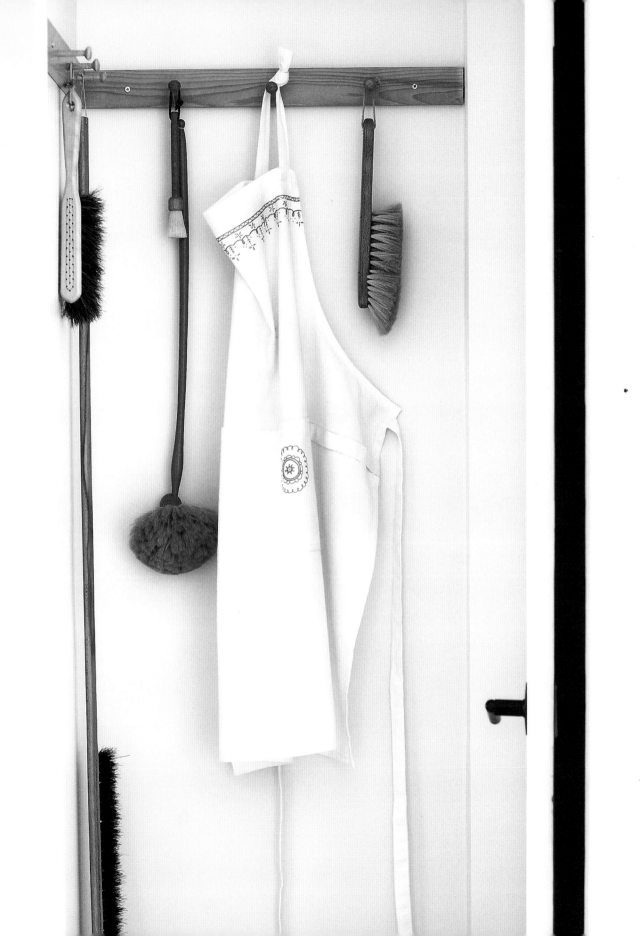

32. Hand towel
/ motifs pages 110-111

33. Place mats
/ motifs pages 112-113

34. Linen pillowcase
/ motifs page 114

35. Jam covers
/ motifs pages 116-117

36. Notebook cover

/ motifs pages 118-119

37. Vase holder

/ motifs page 115

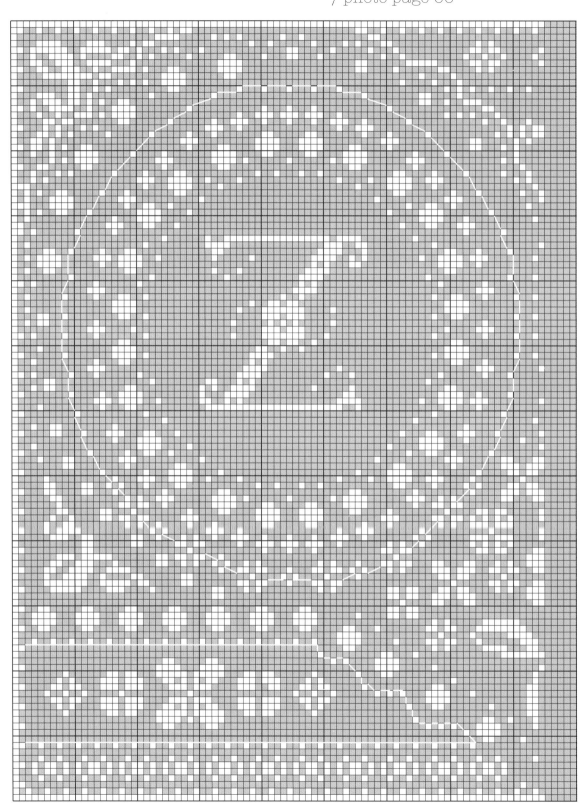

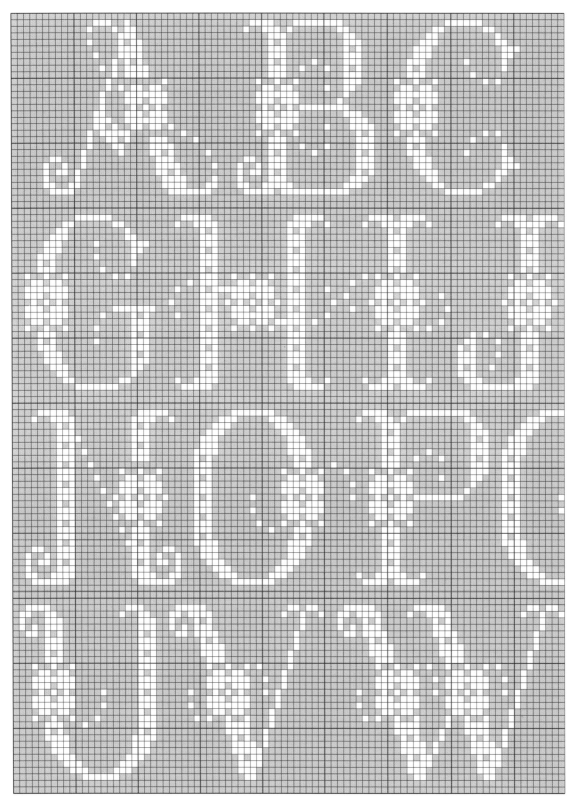

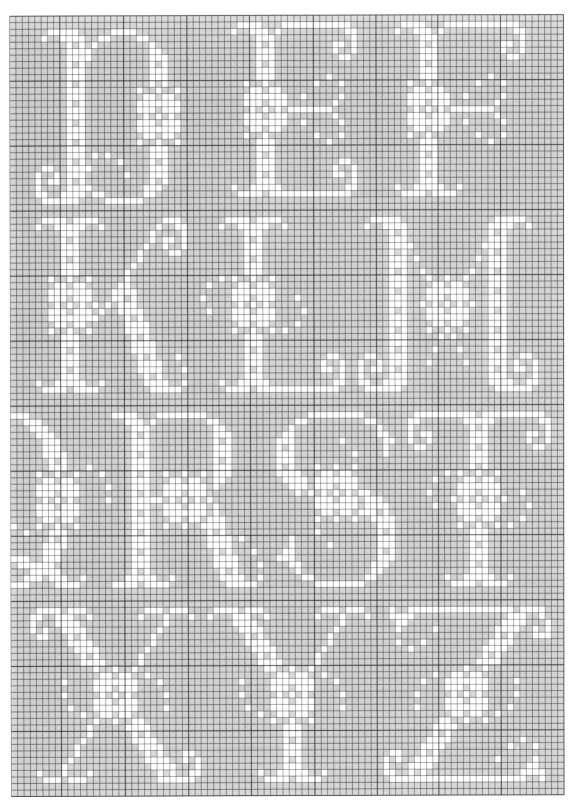

21. Good luck cushions

/ photo page 68

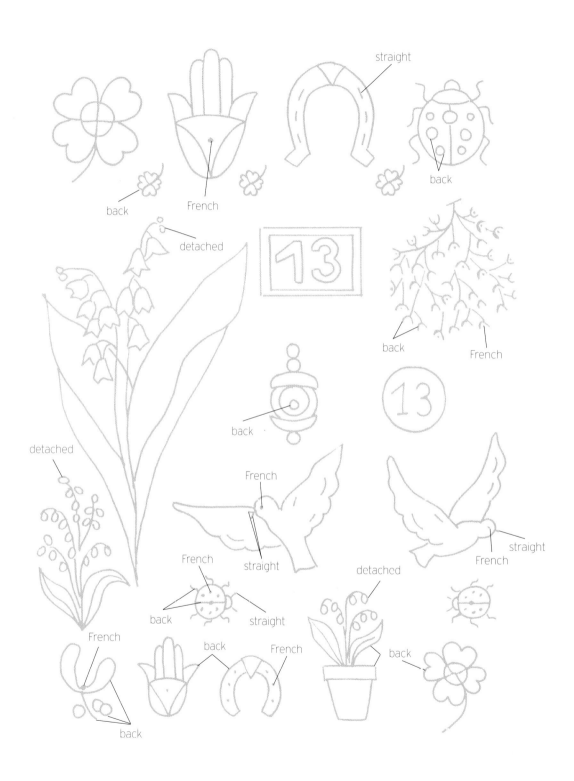

back

French

detached

back

back

French

back

22. Secret notebook

/ photo page 69

French

detached
French
straight
straight

French

back

French

back

French

back

back

back

straight

back

French

back
back

French

straight

back   French

straight

straight

straight

23. Small pictures

/ photo pages 70-71

25. Stole

/ photo page 73

26. Lampshade

/ photo page 74

/ photo page 75

28. Plant markers

/ photo page 76-77

straight

French

straight

straight

straight

French

straight

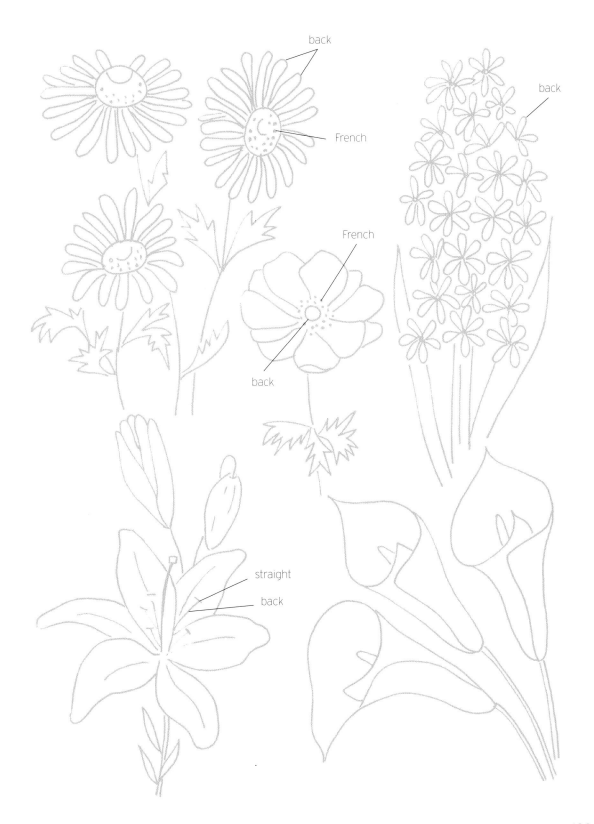

back

French

back

French

back

back

straight

back

/ photos pages 78-79

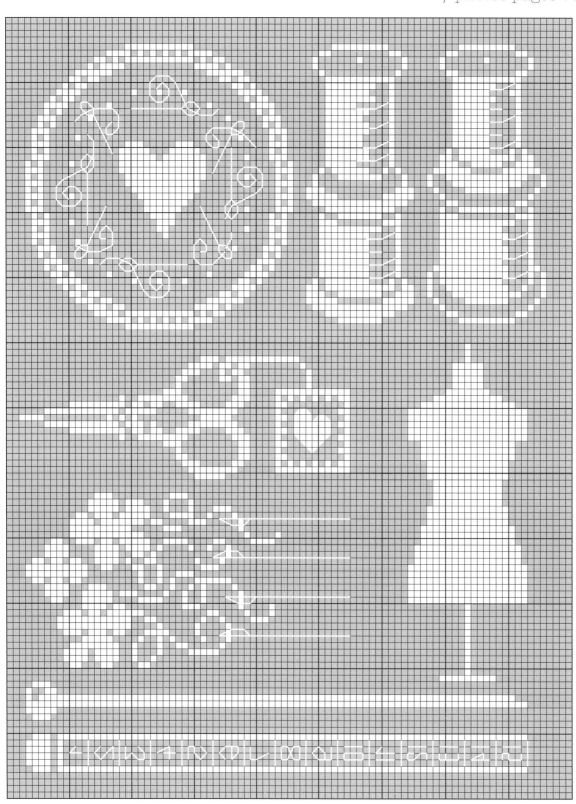

30. Monogrammed tea towels

/ photo page 80

stem

stem

detached

straight

detached

31. Kitchen apron

/ photo page 81

French

detached

back

detached

back

detached

French

detached

French

French

back

French

back

straight

detached

French

French

back

French

back

straight

French

back

straight

detached

back

straight

33. Place mats

/ photo page 83

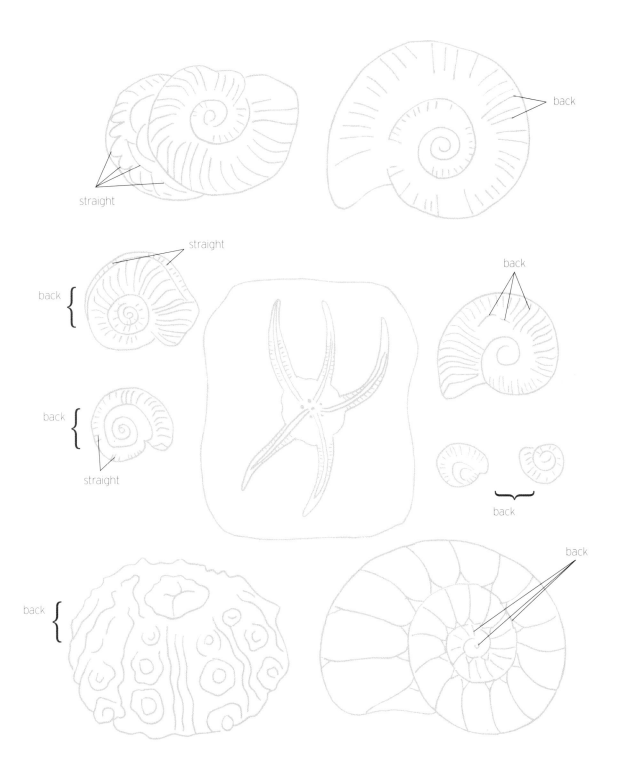

straight

back

straight

back

straight

back

back

back

back

back

34. Linen pillowcase

/ photo page 84

/ photo page 85

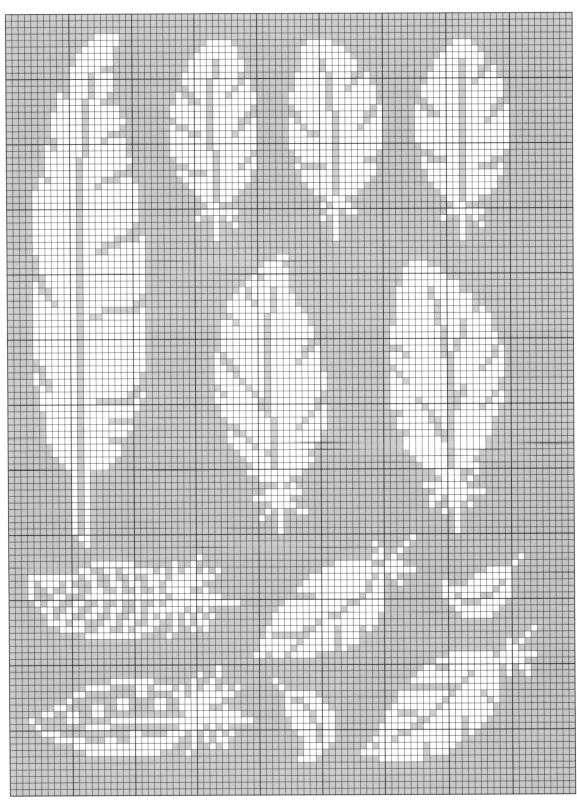

blue

38. Sneakers
/ motifs pages 144-145

39. Alphabet sampler
/ motifs pages 144-145

40. School bag / motifs pages 146-147

41. Travel notebooks
/ motifs pages 148-149

42. Dolls
/ motifs pages 150-151

43. Canvas shoes
/ motifs pages 152-153

44. Smock
/ motifs pages 154-155

45. Tea-time tea towels
/ motifs pages 156-157

46. Table napkins
/ motifs pages 158-159

47. Beach towel
/ motifs pages 160-161

48. Snack bag
/ motifs pages 162-163

49. Samples

/ motifs pages 164-165

50. Singlet top
/ motifs pages 166-167

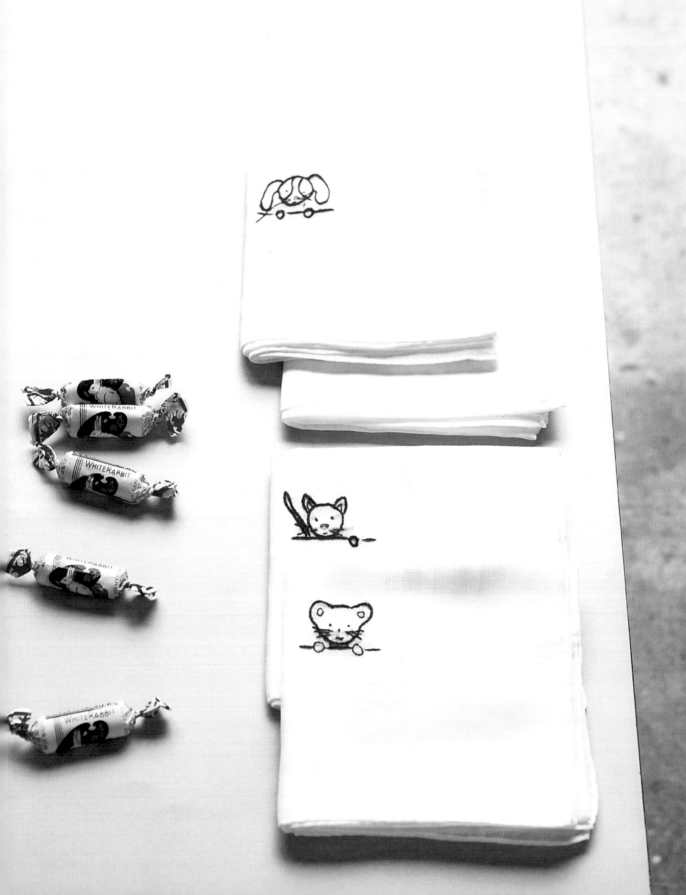

51. Handkerchiefs
/ motifs pages 168-169

52. Bed linen
/ motifs pages 170-171

53. Seaside motifs
/ motifs pages 154 & 172-173

54. Hand bag
/ motifs pages 174-175

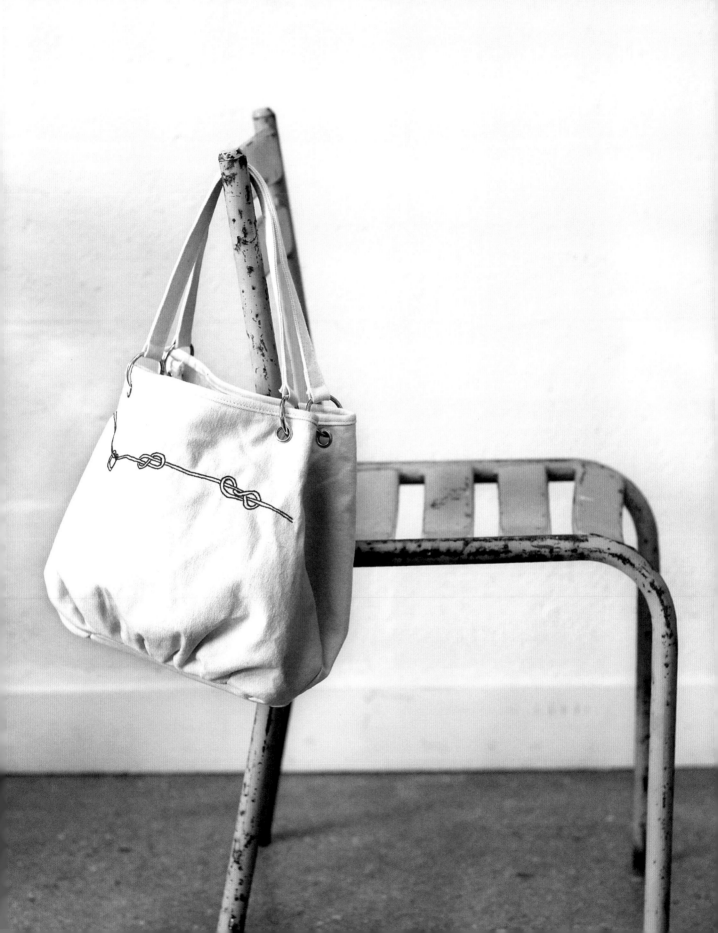

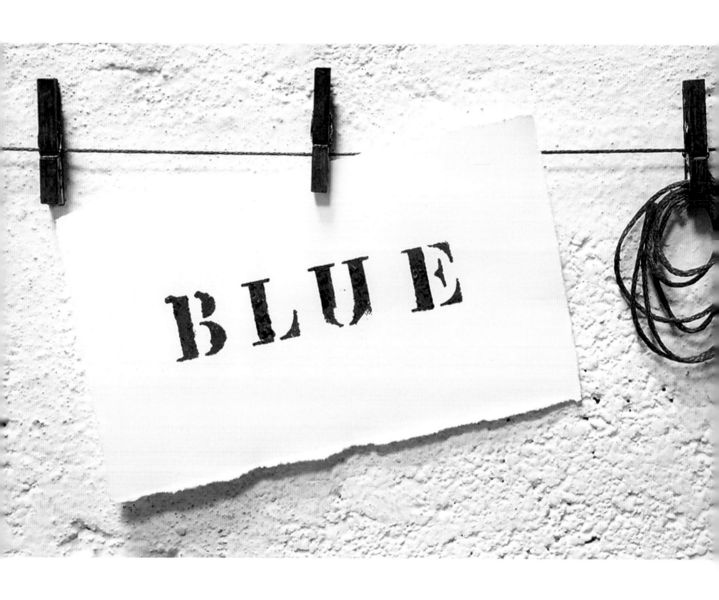

55. Embroidery pocket

/ motifs pages 154-155

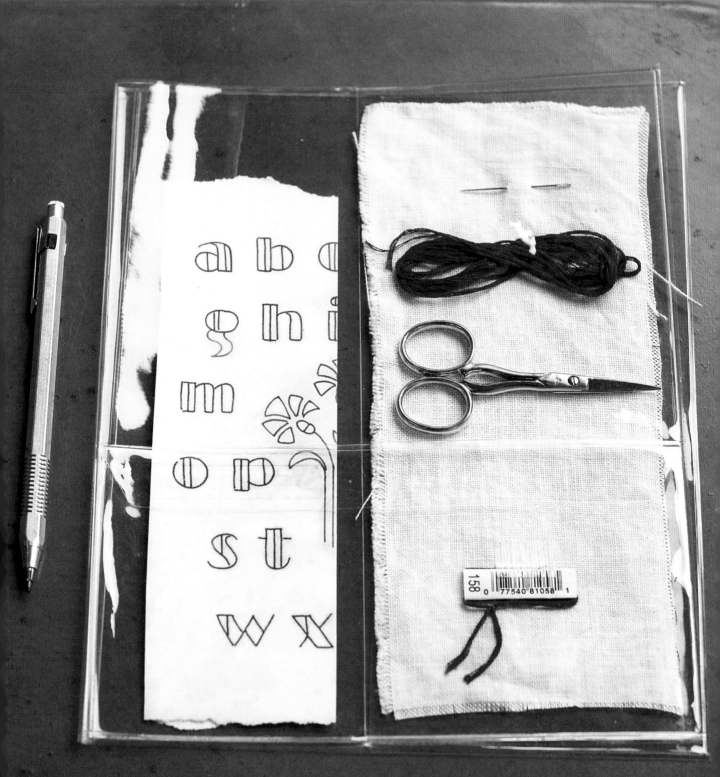

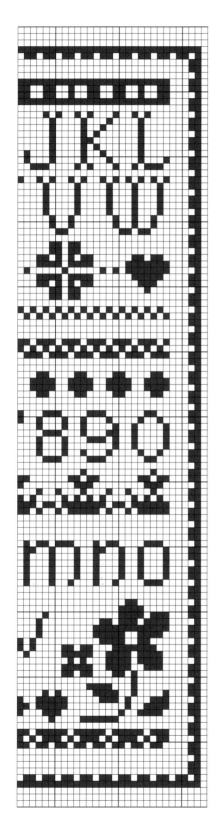

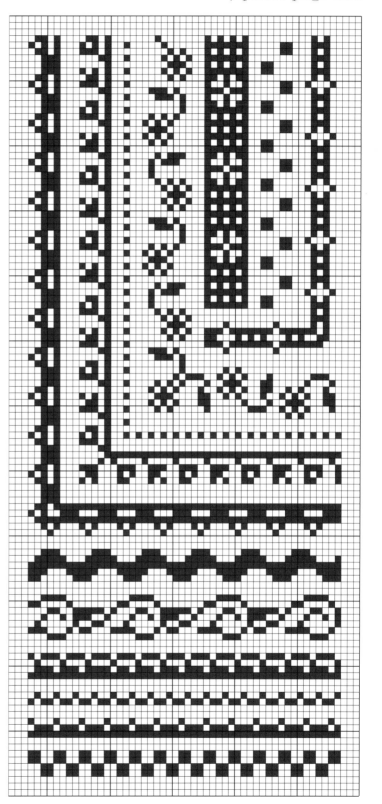

40. School bag
/ photo page 124

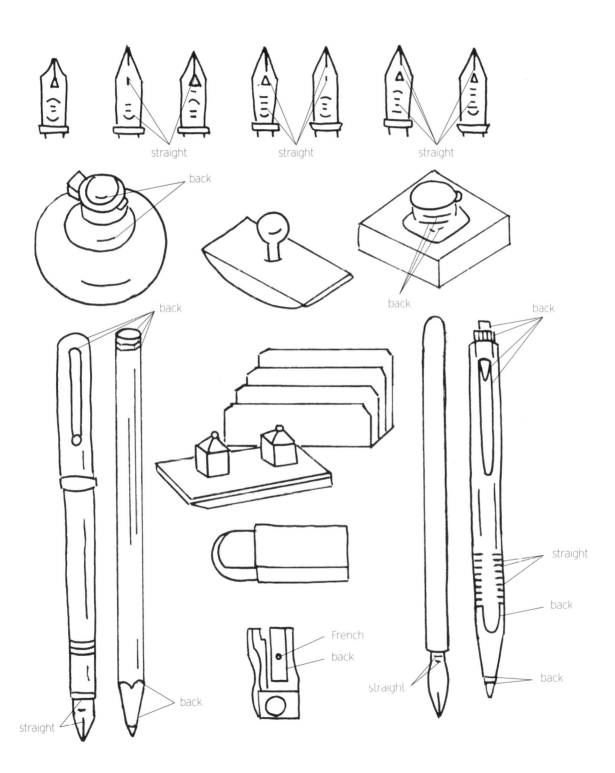

straight

straight

straight

back

back

back

back

back

straight

back

French

back

straight

back

back

straight

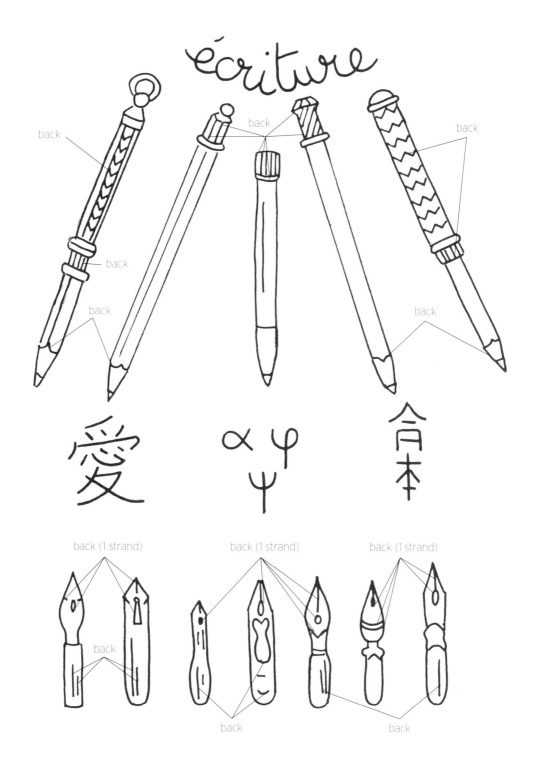

écriture

back
back
back
back
back

back

愛 αΨΨ 合本

back (1 strand) back (1 strand) back (1 strand)

back

back back

42. Dolls
/ photo page 126-127

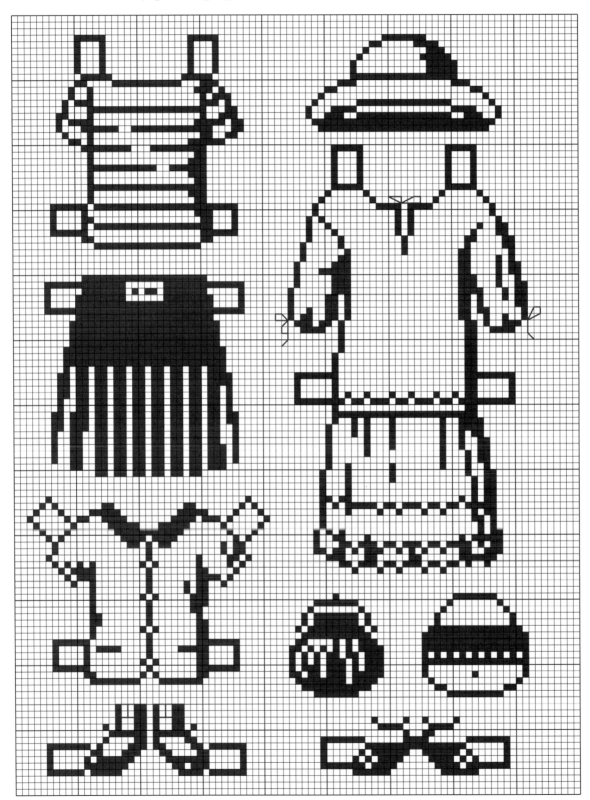

43. Canvas shoes
/ photo page 128

straight

straight

French

straight

back

back

back

back

back

French

back

straight

detached

back

44. Smock
/ photo page 129

back

stem (6 strands)

back

back

stem (6 strands)

stem (6 strands)

stem (6 strands)

/ photo page 130

46. Table napkins

/ photo page 131

back

straight

back

back
French
straight

back
(1 strand)

straight

back

back

back

back
(1 strand)

back

back

159

47. Beach towel

/ photo page 132

48. Snack bag / photo page 133

49. Samples
/ photo page 134-135

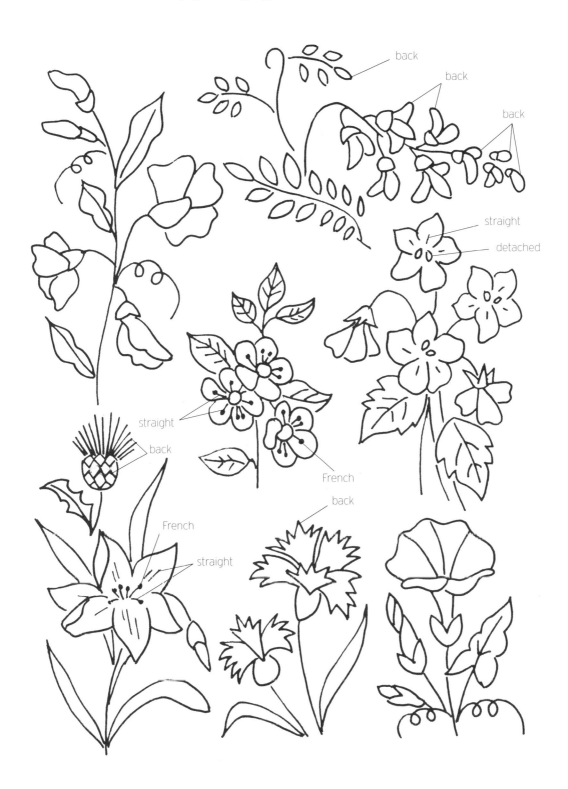

back

back

back

straight

detached

straight

back

straight

French

French

straight

back

164

French

French

straight

French

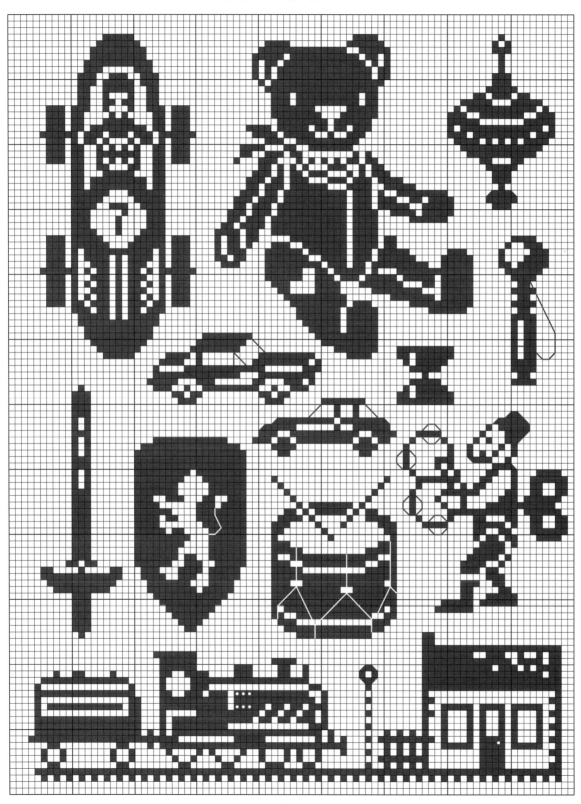

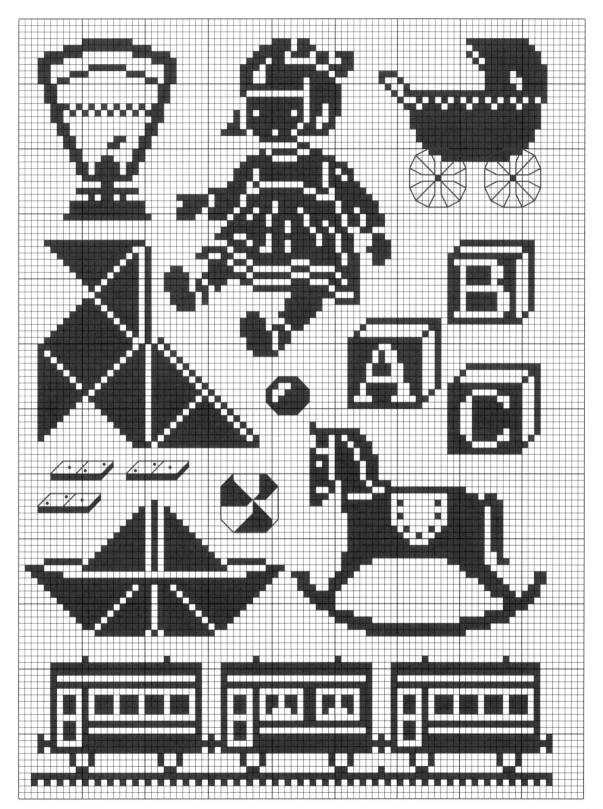

51. Handkerchiefs

/ photo page 138

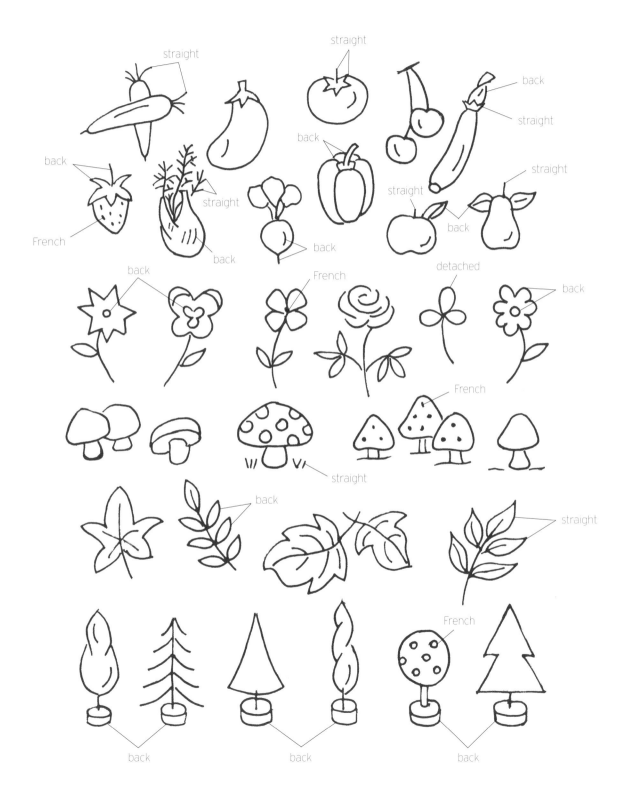

169

53. Seaside motifs

/ photo page 140

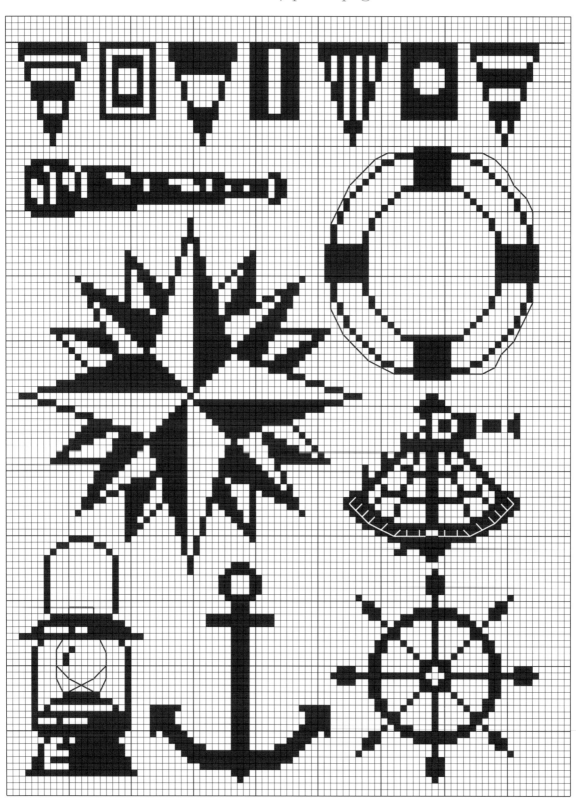

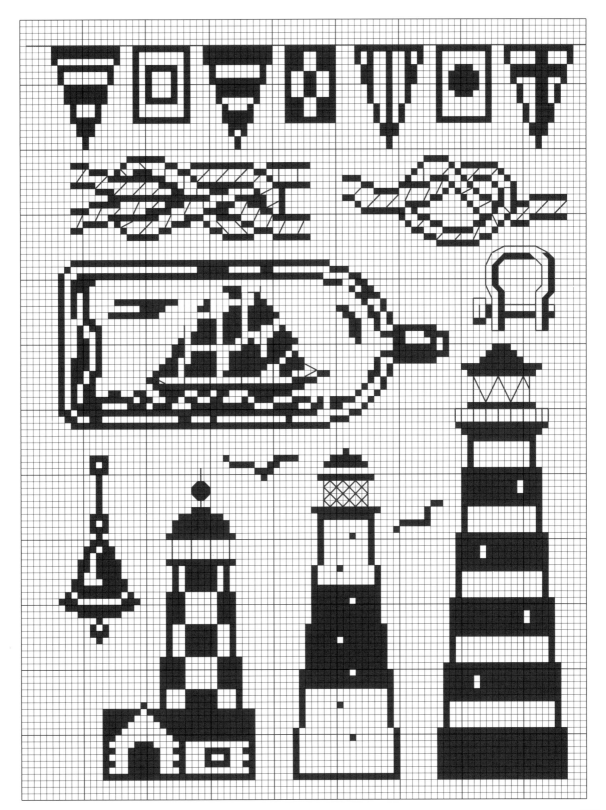

54. Hand bag / photo page 141

French

back

French

straight

straight

back (1 strand)

back

straight

back (1 strand)

back

straight

French

straight

Published in 2009 by Murdoch Books Pty Limited

Murdoch Books Australia
Pier 8/9, 23 Hickson Road
Millers Point NSW 2000
Phone: +61 (0) 2 8220 2000
Fax: +61 (0) 2 8220 2558
www.murdochbooks.com.au

Murdoch Books UK Limited
Erico House, 6th Floor
93–99 Upper Richmond Road
Putney, London SW15 2TG
Phone: +44 (0) 20 8785 5995
Fax: +44 (0) 20 8785 5985
www.murdochbooks.co.uk

Chief Executive: Juliet Rogers
Publishing Director: Kay Scarlett

Project manager: Katrina O'Brien
Production: Kita George

Printed by 1010 Printing International Limited in 2009
PRINTED IN CHINA

Thank you to Christine and Nathalie for their magic fingers...
And thank you to Valérie and Olivier, and Joëlle and Pierre
for the use of their houses.

National Library of Australia
Cataloguing-in-Publication Data

Author: Delage-Calvet, Agnes.

Title: Made in France : cross stitch
and embroidery in red, white
and blue / Agnes Delage-Calvet
and Anne Shier-Fournel.

ISBN: 9781741963861 (pbk.)

Subjects: Embroidery—Patterns.
Cross stitch—Patterns.

Other Authors/Contributors:
Shier-Fournel, Anne.

Dewey Number: 746.44

A catalogue record for this book is
available from the British Library.

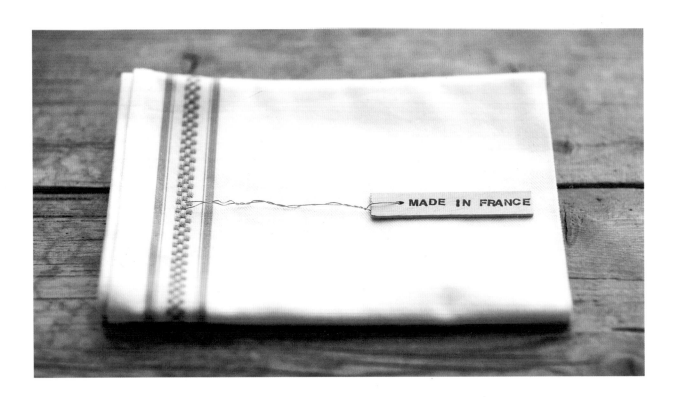